WHO REALLY CARES

Janis Ian

WHO

REALLY

CARES

The Dial Press, Inc.

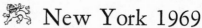 New York 1969

Library of Congress Catalog Card Number: 73–91116
Printed in the United States of America

First Printing, 1969

I don't want to be a poet
I want to change your life

—R. M. RILKE

CONTENTS

JON   *1*

Cock Robin Is Dead   *3*
Mandy In Mourning   *5*
Along the Alley   *6*
Poems for the Young Bedwetter   *8*
With His Crazy Black Hair, Whistling A Breeze   *10*
Poem for the Christening   *11*
Jon   *12*
Horatio   *14*
The Droning Rebels   *16*
79th Street   *19*
Tears   *20*
Poems for the Young Psychologist   *21*
Mama & Me   *23*
Who Comes So Lonely In the Night?   *25*
Philo Judaeus   *27*
Letter to the Damned   *28*
Epitaph   *29*

NEW YORK   *31*

Through These Hallowed Halls   *33*
Poem for the Young Idealist   *35*
Eugene the Crazyboy   *36*
Dirty Dirty Boy   *37*

Poem for a Mundane Sermon　　38
My Sullen Song　　39
Partly at Paul's　　40
Shaving the Turkey　　41
New Christ　　43
By Candlelight In Sullen Night　　44
Aesop's Fables　　45
Hunter　　47
Look / Life　　48
A Chess Player　　49
Lighthouse　　51

PETER　　53

I Love Your Chest Like Cat's Tongue　　55
Song of Surrender　　56
The Arabesque Dancer　　57
A Day In the Circus　　59
This Morning At Sunset　　66
Ambrotype　　68
Bahimsa　　71
Psalms, Psalms　　72
It Is Time We Parted　　74
Analogue　　75
I Am the Lonely River　　76
Like A Lonely Train Wreck, Sneaking　　78
What Then, Eurydice?　　80
The Runes of Atlantis　　82
Christmas Greetings　　85

WHO REALLY CARES

JON

Cock Robin Is Dead

cock robin is dead
who wore a cloak of green
throughout sherwood forest
and stole the huac dream
cock robin is dead
who proudly wore his heart on shoulder
through the crazy splendor of a wounded night
raining
he ran on a cycle through the forest
(just to see how far
was too far)
cock robin is dead whose
madonna wife asked him
why do you laugh?
and was answered
it's you who are laughing
at your reflection in me.
oh yes, he's quite dead
in his black and silver chariot
riding through lonely road
with the night outside
he of amethyst and thyme
cock robin was a quiet fighter
and a hard one to beat

Mmmm cried the mourner
        he of the sister with pale goddess eyes
        shone in the night
        like a chariot of fire
cock robin is dead
who wore a cloak of green
throughout sherwood forest
and stole the american dream

[3]

for a democratic one
    okay!
    (but don't cry yet)
the crucifix is just now being hung
and cock robin is
dead . . .

Mandy In Mourning

Mandy
Who sits in a chair
With her legs in the air
Reaching out for No one
Neither here nor there

And she wouldn't hurt you
She wouldn't touch a fly
If you'd only believe her
Try to receive her
She will welcome you
With open eyes
Mandy bread and butter
Outhouse shelter
Helter skelter

When I was a child
I lived in a fantasy world

Mandy's playing games
And she can't be ashamed
A disgrace!
I'd tell her mother
But I won't breathe a word of it
    to Mandy
With her eyes overflow
    in salt shine seas
Maybe your fault
But probably me

Along the Alley

The night and I, an only child
Walk or fly this lonely time
Above my head a white snow fly
And through the vein into my eye
Her feet are bent, my hands are blind
She took the silver carrying knife
And in a moment touched the sky
All the pain within my life
    lay hidden by the night

        Her face is framed
        in crystal shame
        I see it in the moan
        So many tears
        in so few years
        Spent dying all alone

The singer weeps into the night
His visions spent, his eyes are blind
I try to find some hint of light
But there's nothing there to ease my plight
Still, a song is sung to try
And halt the tears that wring you dry
In prisoner's row you can see a life
    snuffed out by candlelight

        The jailer's cell
        and mine as well
        are bringing back the day
        A dawning light
        to kill my sight
        to burn the tears away

The dancer sways on golden scales
Her body rails the ancient tale
Of everyone who's ever failed
Concessions on a larger scale
To break the binders, never wail
As much as in the city jail
When a T-shirt woman told her tale
And all the dues you'll ever pay
  won't equal what she had to say

    Her skin it glistens
    with perspiration
    I saw it on the dress
    Boy-girl singing
    and pierced ears ringing
    The queen of all the rest

one day mommy came home from the
hospital with a new baby
brother and she said isn't he
darling don't you just
adore your little brother and i said
yes but
when are we trading him in for the new
'71 model

mommy says he is a
sweet little boy and
daddy says he is an
obedient little boy and
auntie says he is a
good little boy and
i say he is a
pain in the ass

teacher said don't you just
adore your little brother he is
always good   so
sweet and gentle don't you just
adore him and i said i
hate him

mom says little brother didn't
wet the bed last night if he is
dry tonight we will give him a
party with presents & cake
& candy & so tonight
i took a cup of water &
wet his bed for him

[8]

mommy says we still love brother
even if he does
soil the sheets even if he does
wet the bed we still
love him so
tonight i
wet my bed too

With His Crazy Black Hair,
Whistling A Breeze

So now he's gone from life
Of his own free will he left — he did
With his crazy black hair flapping in the breeze
As it did when he used to tease
And pretend he was going but
This time, it's no pretending
"He was so bright!"
But there's no time for genius
When you have problems to solve
And crazy black hair to wave in the breeze

Who will wipe the tears away?
Who will hear you cry?
    Who'll pull the knife of hate
    from so young a heart?
Who will take abuse and scorn
And still return for more?
No . . .
Not I
who loved you more than yesterday
respected in the same.
Not I.

Who'll give time to love
When there are problems to be solved
And crazy black hair to wave in the breeze
How will you fare without the breeze
    my love?

Poem for the Christening

They sat quietly by the grave.

"He was such a good boy . . . always so polite." The mother sat silenced, thinking of praise to show how sorry she was. "Such a comfort to me in my old age."

Papa smiled, saying "He was an awfully good ball player." And his almost best friend sat numbly, wishing he could leave but not doing so out of respect for the grieving.

Papa suggested having all of His friends to dinner and discussing their former good times. Mama wanted to have the relatives over and speak of His past life—the things that were important to Him. (bar mitzvah, first day in school, and other like necessities.) She smiled and asked if perhaps they might have a small gathering . . . uh, a quiet party one might say. In His honor, of course, but I'm sure He would have wanted it that way, she said.

Not that we really want to see the relatives, mused Papa, but just the same, it would be nice.

And his almost best friend replied "Let's all of us go home and everyone remember by themselves. No parties. Just carry on." Which was, of course, exactly the way he'd have wanted it.

Once, Jon, I could have told you
    why the nightbird flew by day
    and winter flowers bloomed in may
    and people never seemed to speak
    when they had nothing to say

But hey, Jon — I've grown too young
to sit and cry
Too small to wonder why
All I do today is sit
and laugh the hurt away

    Only
    let me laugh a little longer

Once, Jon, I could have told you
    why open avenues of sound closed all about you
    and "accidental" bullets always found you
    and none of the cheating do-you-inners
    ever had need to doubt you
    the lonely island man could always find you

Once, Jon, I could have shown you
    why women only cried a child's tears
    and laughing boys never felt the fear
    and we weren't deaf, there was
    nothing more to hear
    the sun became, another year

But hey, Jon — I've grown too young
to try and explain
Too small to push away the pain

And all I do today is laugh
the hurting times away

God
if you'd just have laughed a little longer

Horatio sits
Vomiting in a corner
the streets are hollow
save the pain of his laughter
soundless in agony

       come off it, charlie
       fifteen an hour
       no more no less
       what's a body worth?

His eyes explode in one direction
outside in, they speak
only for strength
In red labyrinths,
I enter slowly

       and may God bless YOU
       sonny boy
       she called to the troop leader
       forty-eight and balding
       what does he care?

Looking at the overflow
drawers in his mind
jesus, it must hurt
to go insane

       I can tell you stories
       will you believe me?
       if I should cry
       will you take me?

[14]

and I can laugh!
will you love me?

I tell the story
only too well
Can you believe me?
Will you believe me?

The Droning Rebels

within the deep and misty caverns of the
"home james" politicians
who speak their gutters and cry
jungle jim and boy leap through the trees
in a frantic effort to recall
all the little puddles
suzy and billy
hide and seek
catch me if you can
and everyone laughs
even the prisoner

jimmy dean on his
motorcycle rampage and
kerouac the hipster
gaze down from poets' graves to say
What's become of the younger generation?
angle hearted hipsters of the
beat generation ask
What happened to the o so cool youth?
the tape recorders of the silent generation
think quietly (so quietly)
What has happened to the children?
   but nobody really cares

london town is falling down
as the galleons of america invade with
pointed threats and quiet delinquents.
disciplined hipsters who walk
in a quiet city of dawn
to the insane asylum
and o it's spring again and
the whole world is
shit

Madison Ave. boys spineless
mindless lads with
dictated ideas
make great sofas
or foot stools
or tape recorders

baby's down
shack town
cold green abyss
lights frantic candles as
elderly statesmen leap in the shadows of time
it's summer again
unaffiliated

elderly little old lady suddenly
runs to phone booth and
switches on her secret identity of
elderly little old man
everyone takes it calmly, talking about the
good
old
days every week they talk about the
good
old
days when they were
born they talked about the
good
old
days

snow falling white from sky as
Black Cardiac and New Lace walk to their
more favored cafe thatistosay the
Outsider where they find Square Cat sitting with
Hipsister and the FBI comes
Square Cat waves goodbye as they are
all given dehydrated seltzer for lunch &

subsequently you know die of
gas pains

oh it's summer again and the
pool is filthy as hell
dammit

the sour little old lady crossing
saints boulevard suddenly
looked up and saw
god
being a religious woman she was
violently opposed to fanatics and
naturally went straightforth to the
police who came and shot god
d   o   w   n
everybody knows real gods don't
bleed
christ

white snow falling gently into
ribbon of the deep
heart of hate

Sunday night at the pool hall
i had an uncle tom
retrieve my ping pong
and each time i lost the ball
he bent to receive it
Somehow symbolic
behind the veneer and shuffle
i knew he laughed
much harder than i

Tears

hey — I'm crying, ma
my tears make hard salt crystals
they dissolve in my blood
and I cannot drink cyanide
falling through the hollow heart

it comes quickly now
forming an icy wall
which slowly melts into oblivion
as once before, I stand
unclothed

hey! I'm crying
for the river of time is the bourbon and wine
my tears of cheap wine . . .
tequino makes me laugh

      when you pass by
      and ask me why
      shall I deign to reply?
      what do I own but the tears of my song
      pray, let me show off my wares
      and I say
      a pebble will outlast me
      a grain of sand for the mind of man

if you wish to see me alive then
come quickly
for I feel a kerchief
dabbing at the tears

Poems for the
Young Psychologist

i was going to take a bath
and mommy said dont
overload the tub dont
take too many toys dont
eat the soap
and the tub began to leak
i took too many toys
froze to death and
chewed on the soap
and when she asked where
did you ever get ideas like that
i said i just   dont

we went to stay with grandma and i said
o i forgot my lucky dog
mommy said dear its
old and its hair is
gone and anyway you mustnt be so
dependent
sleep without him
and i said well
you are old
and daddy still sleeps with you

one day i took a rock and threw it at mommy
& it hit the window which
b   r   o   k   e
daddy raised his hand to
hit me but mommy said dont
she'll get a complex
and daddy said sometimes dear you are just
too damned progressive

i was playing truck with jimmy when
daddy said she should play with
dolls not trucks
mommy said let her be she is
self motivated and he said
no and she said
yes and they argued
a lot
so in i went to ask for a
doll instead of a
truck
so theyd stop

we were eating when daddy came
home from a long tiring day and
started complaining how come the
food wasnt hot and the
steak was no good and the
house was all dirty and he
turned to me and
opened up his mouth and
i said
dont take your frustrations out on me
baby

Mama & Me

O mama
I'm bleeding
And you stop up my wounds with cyanide
        you've grabbed from my dreams
        each night
        as I lay there
        thinking of you

O mama
I'm hurting
And you soothe the tears with
Smoke in my eyes
        the smoke you steal
        from the incense I burn
        in filial devotion

O mama
I'm burning
And you cool my brow with
Rags dipped in kerosene
        and you take the rags
        from the sackcloth I wear
        to remind me of you

O mama
I'm dying
And I'll cool your brow
  with my spit
And I'll soothe your wounds
  with my fists
And I'll stop up your tears
  with laughter

[23]

O mama
And when the end comes
Shall we tell them what it means
To interrupt a dream?

Who Comes So Lonely In The Night?

My laughter is the joyfilled hysteria of one
Who laughs to avoid the snapping of his mind
    (Listen—the sound of a room, ticking)

My shame is the shame of a madman
Sorrowed on seeing what he could not help but do
    (Listen to the silence of my song)

My illness is that of the patient
Upon seeing how little time is left
Must needs get it all done quickly
    (You are not deaf
    There is nothing to hear)

My words are the words of one
Who has forgotten his native tongue
    (Listen to the language of our eyes)

My poems are those of a man on an island
Seeking to recapture what once he knew
    (Listen to the rustling of a dead leaf)

My songs are those of the swallow who
Caught in a spiderweb, imprisoned till death
Sings only that he may not be forgotten
    (Watch the gannet in flight,
    How quickly he falls)

My wishes are those of a prisoner who
On seeing what he can't possibly attain
Only yearns for it all the more

(Listen for the sound of a wish on a star
How many stars before the wish can shatter?)

My wants are those of a human
My life is that of a half-woman
And my tears are those of one
Who has nothing left to give
But his sorrow

Philo Judaeus

The river tide is run
Philo Judaeus
your shaken bowl
cannot keep the earth

    No more
        the eyes of God intone
        halt the slaughter of angels
    No more yesterdays
        written plain on parchment
    our kingdom come
    does not exist
    for the likes of us
    No more loving mothers
        Philo Judaeus
        we have been forgotten
  never mind the ecstasy
  hide your sailor's eyes
    they can not save us
    Philo Judaeus
    imagine
No more
    you
No more
    me
Even God is weeping

Letter to the Damned

Year of their lord, soon to be designed
in a pattern of the mind
so much less than rhyme

The second stage having begun, Jeffrey the
Pumpkin Maker wandered out of his car
forcefully. 'What did you learn in school?'
asked the high priestess.

'Ho boy' replied Jeffrey atavistically. 'If the
moon were not so high I should become an
activist.'

'This is something new' said father, sipping
from a genuine tea glass of imported japan.
'Possibly just a face he's going through.'

'Jeffrey laughed with scorn' said the high priestess.

Jeffrey laughed with scorn and replied 'Not so
not so. How long is it since you've seen Jeremiah
. . . or even an angel?'

Finding no reply, he trundled to the car and
turned his back on the future.

Jeffrey the Pumpkin Maker died of eating too many
humanoids next week. The high priestess was
coveted and father left for the mountains to become
a guru. Myself, I wish for Jeffrey the best of luck
and relief from tension or sin.

Hoping you're the same . . .

when the cyclone winds took
air and slapped the sand
     right into
       arab's
       face

when the heaviest sun
added weight to a
     prisoner's
     shovel &
      pick

when the poverty came
and choked just like a
     poor man's
      starched
      collar

jesus had come again
stoned for impersonation
     and sat
      upon the
       open air

NEW YORK

Through These Hallowed Halls

In mourning
    at sunset
we make our way

        through these hallowed halls
        I've been
        searching for the end
           boys in blue ribbon
               surrender my cause

The trees
    are weeping
can't you see?

        sunlight through my hollow prism
           yes, I face the park
       and keep my eyes downcast
          not to be bothered
              at spring

Let me ride!
    (I'll break the walls
nervous tutor)

        yesterday the sun was high
          today it's all in shadows
       would you like to keep me here
         a useful member
           of society?

I should fly to the heights
    of your misery

locked in too long
no wonder I carry
a knife

far better to be swallowed
by the sun
than wallow in darkness
forever

Poem for the Young Idealist

teacher said do you
hate your mommy? i said i
love her and she said you're
lying you don't really
mean that
do you?
i said i'm sorry i
love her and she said i was
very
sick

Eugene the Crazyboy

Hey it's Eugene the Crazyboy!
I wonder is it all an act?

Everyone treats him like thin glass
Don't shout — you'll break it!
Me, I treat him like I do my friends
Don't break — I'm shouting

Eugene doesn't talk so good with strangers
Gives them weird answers or just
doesn't answer at all
And they think it's absurd

> He talks real good to me, though!
> Always smiles
> We talk about horses and government
> and swimming and living and
> just about anything we think of

But when anyone else comes by
He starts to stop

Eugene once gave me a present
A clip-on earring
And I said   Thank you
putting it in my pants
just to prove a point

Eugene the Crazyboy got put away
In a home for sterilised nurses
and an official insanity card
But I'll bet you a five
he never gives them presents

Dirty Dirty Boy

There's an avenue of people
who believe in faith
And the wanderers suffer
'cause they never get made
The cause of this injustice
is a world-wide fake
   In lies told to you
   at school
   on the subway
   "Keep your hands in your pockets
   You'll go blind and insane!"
dirty dirty boy
dirty dirty girl
   keep your hands in your pockets
   you'll go blind and insane!

When the lady is a baby
all dressed up to share
She doesn't disappoint you
by playing it fair
She can't shake her money-maker
if it just isn't there
   keep your hands in your pockets
   you'll go blind and insane!
dirty dirty boy
dirty dirty girl
   her mother would say
   Keep your hands in your pockets
   You'll go blind and insane!

Poem for a Mundane Sermon

It was a topical day in Good Fink George's life. The pun was shining, his roominghouse lovelady took up the rent. All was otherwise a formal state of affairs. The King rose, bumbled down steps, potted with age; made his way to the front whore, opened it, stepped out.

A ram was there complaining as to the rest ban treaty and wondering if there would still be unfound resting. Of course! cried Good Fink George, this will always be! Lady spoke of the surplus new nation problem and he absolved to do something about it immediately.

They set upon him with a mighty roar and ferried him into the castle. Placing a crown of horns upon his head, sitting on the stone in the coroner, they laughed at the Good Fink. He rose the window and raved to the crowd bellow. Outside it was raining fags and dogs. A great fear rolled down his cheek. When the crowd saw the crystal fear they cried Don't spurn the other cheek! and so he didn't.

Making his way backwards, George (the first) began to cry. Upon doing so he felt better and quickly churned aground, spreading his wings long in order to get by them all with their surplus regurgitation problems etc.

It was a topical day in Good Fink George's life.

My Sullen Song

Standing on your microphone
Yes, I use feedback at times
With no audience reaction
Turn up the volume
(Do they hear me now?)
Turn on some more highs
get rid of the lows

  Then stand, try to laugh
  And the sun calls out
    fat chance
  So fall, try to cry.
  The river walks by
    not even staring.

Laugh, go on and drown
Funny isn't it?
How many sessions it takes
Before anyone hears the final mix.
You could scratch your eyelids all day
And the tape would run on.

  Then stand, try to sing
  And the wind calls out
    forever trying
  Fall down, laughter rings
  The sun ambles by
    not even smiling

And it's a long
  long time
since the last god died

There's a party in the ballroom.
Everybody's got their gowns on
Drinking a toast
to the hostess and host
of the evening.
My friend the armadillo
was wearing all her grease.
The slumming eccentric
went up to see the Priest
Who along with Beethoven
was sick, to say the least.

Mister Jones he stood with Lonely
and talked beyond his reach
The sequined Star of yesteryear
stood clicking with her knees.
But it's all right, Toulouse-Lautrec,
it's only you and me
Laughing in the doorway at the freaks.

Shaving the Turkey

Don't kid yourself
Reality is their excuse
For anything unpleasant

      for war
      and hate
      and riots
      and newark

Go out and hop a train
Pay your dues
Thirsty boots
Oh for the glory of a depression

      when everyone lived the dream
      of better days to come

Affluent is what we are
Rich as hell and probably
We'll die that way
With a little luck
I'll go to heaven
and start a rebellion

      or possibly they, too, have a statute
      forbidding advocating the
      violent overthrow of
      government
      I wonder if God has any
      interior motive

Everything is realized in the night these days
The day succeeds the night

which succeeds in
making a fool of itself
And I myself succeed the day
ha
ha
I'm drowning

New Christ

New Christ Cardiac Hero
Yes, he's very strong
But once it falls
He'll never rise again

Lonely One lurks on my shoulder
Clutching teddy bears to his heart
He'd like to sleep with mama
But it's common knowledge she was
Dead
      before his conception

And Pro-Girl, she's at the door again
It would be easy to buy her
Maybe even love her
But I'd only be elevating myself

        Baby's got the blues again
        She's taking off her boots again
        She's climbing into bed again
        She's laying down her head again
        The neighbors think she's frigid
        But it hurts her most of all

By Candlelight In Sullen Night

By candlelight in sullen night
I weave a cloak of dreams
On seatossed foam I swim alone
None else may touch the seams.
That none may aid me in my quest
Nor interfere with dreams,
I keep my sleeping hours hid
With coverlets unseen.

The portals of my mind
Are opened to those few
Who see my seamstress hands as blind
And realize I know, too.
But me I cheat on time
By sleeping far too fast
That none may gently wake and find
These dreamers' hands at rest.

It seems that I, the shroud-maker,
Would be lone and far away
Wandering by lone seabreaker
Looking for the easier way
Trusting none but the one
In charge of twilight dreams.
Yet I am keeper and shaker
Of worlds forever, it seems.

So then. Be quick to snuff a light
And let the darkness ease your plight.
Unlovely pen, sketch me a life
By candlelight in sullen night.

I am no stranger to tears
My life flows by
The rivers cry
As I die
      hoping that my makeup
      will cover up the fear
      hoping my new clothing
      will keep away the tears
Saying to you
'Oh nothing, really
There's too much smoke in here'
Running off to powder my nose
at the party

I am no stranger to lonely
Sitting in my one-celled room
Waiting for the nightly doom
Take me
      wishing, had I time to think
      about the world of time
      wishing, had I time to blink
      and stop, for just a while
As I crawl behind the jukebox
of a restaurant

I am no stranger to fear
Walk through the rain
Look for a train
Take me away
      praying that my fear
      will hide itself in darkness
      praying that my fear
      will think it's only loneliness

Creeping toward the moon
and coming home

Yes but I am a stranger to love
Sit in the room, hugging my knees
Laughter shines at memories
You bring to me
       hoping for the sunlight
       to smile at me through dawn
       hoping for the shadows
       to take your place and form
Crawling from my room
and to your bedside

Hunter

So die a slow death
Hunter
Indian warriors will sing your anthem
Over the burial ashes
We will send you off
All silver and gold
Rubies in hand
A smile on your face
For all the secrets we'll never know

Party night back at the old corral. Young superstar Bertha Shlock arrives late (5 min EST) in a flurry of apologies and general talk about lack of sleep due to night work. Then came the introductions, the shaking of cold slimy fish hands but everyone was smiling and so it was O.K. boyo.

Animal Keeper (in charge of looking after superstar's mind and collecting 20% of each nervous breakdown) came with a young man. Of indeterminate age and undefined coloring, he blended into the walls about as well as could be expected.

Hallo SS   he shouted (abbreviated superstar)
Belt up steaming nit   she replied, coughing ectoplasmically.
But Bertha baby, here is the reporter from Teen Scream Magazine.

TS: Miss Shlock, does the artist reflect the society around him?

BS: Yeah? then I'll start mass-producing chaos.

All this was taken down on an eight-track machine, it would later be mixed and sent over to the HUAC Commission on Civil Rights. The HUAC-CCR was concerned at present with the take-over of the Industry by a band of youths calling themselves "Genuine Artists of Creation" who were handled expertly by William Morris agents.

Party night back at the old corral, young superstar Bertha Shlock rapidly succumbing. In the end she was tired but everyone was still smiling so she guessed it was O.K. boyo and then with laughter in her eyes was carried screaming from the room.

[48]

A Chess Player

The aged are our dearest friends
for only they may teach us
      to comply; with gratitude
the weary soul, bereft of man
            stumbles once again.

                  Someday, shall I live forever?
            (weakness of the flesh)
                  I envy not the setting sun
                        for rising once again.
            Never having had the time
                  to own a memory,
            I see my soul a living shell
                  of dubious quality.

To meet a blue and orange man! yes,
that is all I need — to meet
      a man with glowing eyes, a man
      with blood-red eyes
            (and yet
            I am most satisfied to own
            a dog, who cares for me)

Someday, shall I speak of youth?
      or age, which comes upon us
      as a writer to the pen—
            in time of famine, all honesty
            runs silently aground.
Giving of her teat as much
a farmer to the lamb
            Then lets the blow fall, silent
            upon the door of time.

But then, I will be young again
the living soul has told me
how does one begin to die
without a trace of life?

Lighthouse

I live in the country of the blind
They call me "gifted"
with sight
Yet their hands move faster
than the eye can see

I live in a house of the blind
but my room is darkest of them all

PETER

I Love Your Chest Like Cat's Tongue

I love
your chest
like cat's tongue
    ready for the feast
    and also the
fur
like cat's fur
coiled and waiting I love
your hands
a parrot-wing
brushing the dust off
    my corpse
o to be with you
    forever
in our cat's house of
    clay
I love your
ears like
cat's ears
    prickling my
    every sound
    to see your
nails like
cat feet
dart across my back
    dearest but
    most of all I love your
eyes
like cat's eyes
glowing
    after the feast

Song of Surrender

I wish I were a snowbird
Sitting in a tree
     laughing wholehearted
     nothing bothers her
     cool as a ruffled pigeon feather
     she flies alone
     no V-formation status symbol here
veteran of death
loneliness won't save you
     she flies so easy
wafting through my yesterdays
I found a marker
on the day we killed love
     but better to laugh
     on the day of mourning
     and sing my song to evening
     like a snowbird at twilight
     than spend my days questioning
     the evening silence

The Arabesque Dancer

Naked in swirls
All bathed in curls
The arabesque dancer wheeled about
And gathered kings
(Such pretty things)
Then quickly, shut them out

Her flaming hair
And shoulders bare
Have many a man caught unaware
And captured more
With shining lure
Than nature can—
And kept them there

> "In the sea I writhe,
>   My body bright
>   In cold delight of mystery.
>   With the sea I cry
>   For the pale moonlight
>   And morning's eye to comfort me."

There are no words
For what we hold
Though many men have tried
So may we love
And try to stem
The quickly drowning tide.

Then put no marker on my grave
But leave me with your touch
For the sea I cry

For the ocean, die
And none may say as much

Shed not a tear for you and me—
It can not make us more
And cast a shadow to the sea
The bravest of us all

      "Accept from me
       A fond caress.
       For just a moment, stay
       And give to me
       In tenderness
       The blessings of the blessed."

Then stop.
The tragic willow weeps.
And hold me to your breast
For I am the arabesque dancer
And know your loneliness.

So wipe the pity from your eyes
And raise the questioned glass on high
So say to me, my own delight
     "To us, the rising tide."

A Day In the Circus

1

hie, the lonely river
tenement studies in death
manchild, live beneath the sodden earth
surrounded by
the living dead

Well then dear what **do** you enjoy?

Red-rock sand and
bricks
the Polynesians . . .

summer lay in leisure
gnats
upon the pavement
reeking silence

What's that you say?
Speak quickly
I have no time
The Club awaits me

there are no yesterdays
no future hope
there is only
          today
forever

A child must believe in God
what else can we hold dear?

Bed-rock sand
red bricks
the Polynesians . . .

don't you see the wind
upon your shoulder
can you see his eyes?
did you hear —
God become a parody

2

ahh
the circus tent
keeps a dream
for many

       oooohhh the snake lady
       writhes in simulated flesh
       Daddy will you buy me
       gee I only wish
       would you buy me
       a cobra, Daddy
       I do so love the snake
           He's come at last
       with his pointed head
           venom full
       and beady eyes
           stand erect
           am I yet a child
           to cower before Eden?
       Daddy if you buy a snake
       my very own
       I'll show it to my friends
           take it away!
           take it away,
           Daddy I don't want it
           anymore!

      God   the pain
he's cute
in a funny way
      don't come any closer!
      please
         don't hurt me
O thank you Daddy,
thank you!
      Deliver me, God
      unto death

  3

the hunchback dwarf
taps his hands
against the wall
forever

      His head
      was fragile stalked
      grotesque
         Simon
         looked like that
         when born
      a parody
      of God
         yet three days later
         resembled nothing more than
         a vacant hole
      but aren't we all?

don't be scared t' laugh folks
he can't hear you

         Simon
         heard me
         when I screamed

  [61]

oh he's been de-manned
miss
don't you be afraid, now

> **Simon**
> **my son**
> **was this to be your life?**

4

the fat man
and his coterie
are on parade each day
from noon to twelve
hear before your very eyes
their conversation

> Haarrryyy she whines
> and whines
> what manner woman this?
> to weigh so little
> in the scheme of man

> > **Think he can shame me?**
> > **that hulk**
> > **I—I am more beautiful**
> > **with my ribs askew**
> > **each day**
> > **from noon to twelve**
> > **it's me that draws a crowd**

> surely she must eat
> how then does she lose it?
> she is gnarled and ugly
> and hates me

> > **Harry!**
> > **your shoes**
> > **the crowd is laughing**

[62]

puffing his hands
scrabble for the earth
and fall backwards
on the ground

hahahahahahaha

      Am I thus ashamed?
      to do my laces before you
      Ah, the weight of misery
      hangs a body low
      Stifles the bone sure as
      lard

          If I had a man
          to take me away

      Had I a woman
      fragile as the sea
      to adore

          Harry? and I?
          you must be kidding ?

      jesus god
      what do you want?
      who would take me as I am
          save her?

what a riot!
did you hear?
they're getting hitched
it's all over town

      She will suck my venom
      She will take my veins
          and suck the body through

She will take my livelihood
out of petty jealousy

Him? he'll be on top
like he's always wanted
and me, I'll be crushed
as I've always wanted

5

evening
the wedding bells toll
in silence
forever

these are the walls
the walls,
ever pressing down our
fellow man

Well if you don't like it
go get somebody else

Is this the death of hope
the end of pain?

Sure, and you bought her
a snake
When you know very well
they scare me to death

If I'd known then
all I dare not think of now

What do you think I am?
a sewer
to take your drippings?

[64]

Deliver me, Lord
a silent death

What the hell do you want?

> *Red-rock sand*
> *bricks*
> *the Polynesians . . .*

here are we in summer
the gnats
suffocating a parody of God
from parody
    a God

This Morning At Sunset

This morning I cried again
(though only with sorrow)
No one
    saw the tears run down
No one
    felt the racking sob
And I alone wept
for all the tears
ever lost in the nap of time

> *There's no fun being in the spotlight*
> *when no one is looking*

This afternoon I screamed
(though only for effect)
No one
    saw my hands upon the rafters
No one
    heard my body shake the walls
And I alone shouted
for all the hands
we let go unnoticed

> *How do you count to ten*
> *if you haven't any fingers?*

This evening I died again
(though only with laughter)
No one
    read my epitaph
No one
    gave black orchids
And I alone

as only I can be
laughed softly through the tears

It's no fun dying
if no one sees

Ambrotype

Politics? o man
you flatter yourself
to venture an opinion . . .
and you're so unready for war.
political machinery
you bow and scrape to;
all the while the dribble
spills down your chin
clouding your eyes
o man
you flatter yourself to think
even in non-spatial terms
and I wish
you wouldn't impose
your lack of human relations on me

Plasticine Cardboard Cutouts
I came out of the womb
standing when you pressed
tabs A and B
dead I became a piece of earth
and in my furrow of innocence
nourished a maple tree
becoming part thereof
I shielded a rock from rain
and was warm in knowing
it loved me.

carrion of death
wed-winged, soar into the sun
I feel the rising tide within me
anger I'll rip you to pieces!

[68]

anger I'll scream and shout!
anger we'll make the world over!

(foolish carrion)
when your wings are dead
from the beat of innocence
can you fly?
when your throat is ripped from the breast
like spawn from the mother lode
do you whisper truths in a monotone?
when the world is made over
will there be room enough
for you to sit still?

bubbling sand
I built a castle by the sea
made of glass
fragile as the wind
and when night rushed in
to take my castle
I was enclosed therein
        picture, if you will
        my being
        carried out to sea
        in a trifling moment
as the castle was rent
the sea
washed my body clean

mr. henry finch esquire III
your sense of righteous indignation
overwhelms me
with your multimillion dollar wife
and your golden pennies children
ashine in fool's gold
you 'deplore the plight of the wretched poor'
mr. henry finch esquire III

your sense of righteous indignation
overwhelms me

sitting in a doorway
you wallowed in degradation
I didn't mean to help you
raise the bottle to your lips!
just wanted to befriend
someone quite as drunk as I—
and share a few memories
I never meant to be you
I only meant to help you
but have I any choice?

death   whose
hunger transforms me to animal lust
do not crave my soul
and leave the body to rot
in a furrow of steel
I shake my fist at you, death
for taking what I had
and returning far less
I spit at you death
for breaking my nerve
and leaving the bones
I laugh at you, death
without the decency
to capitalize your name
I pray to you
        for taking my soul
        and leaving the knowledge

Bahimsa

When the lilacs of his eyes
turn to chutes of the assassin
    and come hurtling down
When the lilies of his youth
turn, fading and brown
When the hourglass of his mind
turns, bleeding and bound
All the roses of his dreams
lie scattered
    upon the ground.

When the flowers of her lover
have turned to flowers
    of the grave
When his caressing lips
have turned from red to grey
When flowers burn, only
memories remain
His silver medals turned to dust
and an ashen marker
    is made.

When a wind from Hiroshima
blows ashes
    into the town.
When they slowly sift to form
a blanket, upon the ground
When the earth turns to a tomb
no flowers can be found
And the silken mantle he wore
has turned
    into a shroud . . .

Psalms, Psalms

psalms
psalms
hunger is cumulative
and anger contagious
keep away from churches kid

choirs
benches
the old people sit in the park
the young people lie on the grass
keep back from the ages kid

grey
brick
the old buildings are crumbling
the new held together by glue
stick to the middle of the street kid

sun
clouds
the sky being overcast looked at me
I being undercast saw the sun
carry a lightning rod at all times kid

lies
stories
everything they told you was true
and everything they proved was a lie
don't take up metaphysics my boy

laugh
sing
without love where would we be

back in the garden of eden
an apple a day lets you pray boy

so
so
that's the way your life runs
plastic smooth as plastic
don't you think I know kid?

It Is Time We Parted

this morning
at dawn
I wakened dead
to all natural resources
the blundering hulk beside me
a burnt out husk
of former affairs

my friend   said I
it is time we parted

and he watched with naked eyes
as I packed my bag
and ran for life
to the home of my wanton lover
my own

Analogue

your train
        in
my canyon
            asleep
            on a bed of rails
hurdle
up and down
        I've jumped
        the track
one too many times
                have you been there
                before?
touch
listen
        your train
            greases
        my rails
smooth riding
            have I been
            before?

the sunset depression
everyone knows
but what of the morning sky?
        my bird
            would fly
                for you

I *Am the Lonely River*

I   I am the queen of crimson violet blushing
loneliness
and hold the title well
I am the king of black magic
emptiness
(king of satire
ruler of none)
the crown wears easy on my brow
jack of all trades, I am the master sailor
and can fix your vessel in no time
my dear

let the river tell me what I
    already know
that the jack of diamonds is gone
may his shadow hang low
on my brow
as if to mock our sterile setting
calmness runs over.

my cup anointed,
I surrender captain
take me; willingly
I submit

and if they should ask
    what became of her?
    (those foolish wagging tongues)
merely say
I have shrugged my shoulders with the best of men

II   I am the lonely river
and know no bound'ry

save the shoreline
obedient to the whim of selfish matter
I flow and ebb
consumed by his might
    is this too much to ask of time?
when he beckons
come forth
and on release, sink gently
into my cradle of earth

III   I shall take what I want
and a pox on your revelations!
    (we hear no music, you and I
    but for god's sake
    save the stars)
footloose as I
shoeless as I
the king is dead.
live long in memory

IV   staving hunger
kaleidoscope excels my rate of speed
the shadow moves
too quickly to be seen
    and night
    spent
    raining on my window

Like A Lonely Train Wreck,
Sneaking

Structured in safety
The poet reeks of hollow song
cutting a heartache
snipping the memory
we have left
        (ta-ta-ta)
    your paper doily

                When was I young?
            There were parties.
            Paper doilies.

        False poet—
                one day per year
                acknowledge your birth
                in parties
                        Paper doilies

Do you arouse
the women we meet,
and push away their tears?

                I find no grave
                for pain
                Nor final resting place
                with wooden box
                and paper masque
                It will haunt you
                        forever.

must you be so insipid?
those afraid to feel

        [78]

will buy your name
            will turn the page
            reading aloud to a favorite cat
            buying puppy dogs
            for company

Harbinger of easy love—
I will haunt you
      forever.
      You mock traditions of the heart!
      You—both blessed and damned.
                  a cardboard train
                  soot-ridden
                  covers the desert
                  is this the only train?
                        let us climb aboard
                  rather soot than hunger
                        let us climb aboard
                  Don't ask when the next train stops!
                        rather, climb aboard

Take me for an easy ride—
I will haunt you
      forever.
you are tired
too tired
      wish me well, fellow muse
      have I so much time?
build the bridges high.
Now. Let us surrender.
      let us buy our cats and dogs
      as we climb aboard

What Then, Eurydice?

I   And if I should die before you sleep
What then, Eurydice?
Will you force a tear down the ridge
to please me
as I lie there, teasing you with life?
Bend low to hear my gasping breath
shortened at last
by space
        Infinity
        has always been my name

II   Solder the coffin tight, mother.
Don't forget—
        we have a habit to maintain
Bury the dead without your grief
they cannot hear.
        Only a till of sod in life
        I am the living sky

III   Don't let the children
call my name in their sleep
I fear it will wake you
God knows
we tried hard enough
to teach you life
Sleep.
        your dark imprisonment
        comes too soon before the light

IV   Be not ashamed, Eurydice
        for the sky to carry my longing.

Be not ashamed, Eurydice
    of the lonely stranger
    death

The Runes of Atlantis

I see
the city, rising
like a broken vessel
upon the waters of my disbelief

      Mothers who play in the park
      bring children to console themselves
          wait! wait!
          you'll have children too someday!
      go on run around fall down break-a-leg
          hah. then you'll learn

the old men
the dead men
and trees
with gnarled and broken branches
spent, reaching for the sun

          After the red rubber ball, Nicky!
          Catch it quick!
      Ooo you're gonna get it when
          papa finds out . . .
          conditioned fear
          a reflex emotion
      teach your children;
          their energy spent
             reaching for the sky

Like a tombstone graveyard
my mind is an inscription
left behind by
      oblivious corpses

As kings are killed by princes
neverending.

    Zowee cor just look at 'im bleed
        never seen such a sot in m' life
    where's he from
        & what's he done
            forever and for more?

                your children learn in school
            when you kill the power
            for the throne
            beware!
                and stop your brother's moan

    the young girls
        carelessly sun themselves
    young boys
        carelessly intrude
            spinning mad circles
                through destiny

but I can not love their jellied limbs
        broken, in careless ecstasy
I can not love their withered smiles
        nor can I grieve for this, my own
        laid out before the sun

        Oh my God
            Is it so ugly
                to have tried and failed?
    (no one comes near you
        ever again)

for countless prisons have I wrung
        the sweat, in beads
        from off my tongue

    [83]

of too much bitterness installed
too much pain
   too much gall

            So laugh! the park
                  is filled with trees
            and let the silent mourners file
                  slowly past
            Children, come!
                     join in the play!
                  (*you'll die to dance
                     another day*)